DATE			

AND **100** BOOKS

Also by Mary Leonhardt

Parents Who Love Reading, Kids Who Don't
Keeping Kids Reading

99

WAYS TO GET KIDS TO LOVE READING

AND 100 BOOKS THEY'LL LOVE

MARY LEONHARDT

Three Rivers Press
New York

Copyright © 1997 by Mary Leonhardt

Published by Three Rivers Press, 201 East 50th Street, New York, New
York 10022. Member of the Crown Publishing Group.

Random House, Inc. New York, Toronto, London, Sydney, Auckland
http://www.randomhouse.com/

THREE RIVERS PRESS and colophon are trademarks of Crown
Publishers, Inc.
Printed in the United States of America

Design by Mercedes Everett

Library of Congress Cataloging-in-Publication Data
Leonhardt, Mary.
    99 ways to get kids to love reading and 100 books they'll love /
by Mary Leonhardt.
        p.   cm.
    1. Reading.   2. Children—Books and reading.   3. Reading—
Parent participation.   I. Title.
LB1050.L452   1997
372.4—dc21   96-51711
                                                           CIP

ISBN 0-609-80113-9

10   9   8   7   6   5

CONTENTS

Part II: 100 Books They'll Love

ACKNOWLEDGMENTS

Special thanks to all the parents, teachers, and librarians who have talked to me and written to me about their problems and successes with reading.

Always, special thanks to my family for their support.

INTRODUCTION

When I first started teaching high school English over twenty-five years ago, I thought that avid readers developed their love of books all on their own. Yes, they probably came from homes with book-loving parents. Yes, they were read to as young children. But outside of that? Perhaps they had some book-loving gene that made them immediately see the magic and wonder of reading.

I was wrong. I know now that most avid readers have parents who did very specific things to nurture a love of reading in their children. I've also found that there are very specific things I can do as a teacher to develop avid readers. The things I've found to do aren't rocket science. They are commonsense measures, but they work.

I've presented these reading-friendly ideas as tips in

this book, with only the barest amount of explanation. If you are interested in reading about these suggestions in more detail, I suggest reading my earlier books. *Parents Who Love Reading, Kids Who Don't* focuses on ways of getting very turned-off children and teenagers reading again. It also contains an extensive bibliography of books recommended by my students, including their comments on why they liked the particular books. *Keeping Kids Reading* is based on interviews with my top readers. They explain the kinds of experiences they had that brought them to love reading. I then analyze the kinds of books they liked and describe four different pathways that avid readers seem to follow, depending on their tastes.

This current book is a distillation of those first two, with a number of additional suggestions.

I'm always very happy to hear from readers with either suggestions or questions. You can write to me c/o Crown Publishers, 201 East 50th Street, New York, NY 10022, or e-mail me at maryl@tiac.net

MARY LEONHARDT

Ten Reasons Why We Must Help Our Kids Love Reading

1 Kids have to love reading to become excellent readers. Only if they love reading will they spend lots of time reading. Practice is everything.

2 Avid readers acquire a more complex sense of language. They speak better, write better, and deal better with complex ideas.

3 Reading gives children wide-ranging frames of reference, which make all learning easier. Even children who read only fiction will pick up facts about history, geography, politics, and science.

4
By high school, only avid readers will have the literacy skills to excel in any course that demands a good deal of reading—in other words, in any top-level English, foreign language, history, or science course. They are the kids in the honors classes, the kids who score high on the SAT exam, the kids who have a shot at attending top colleges.

5
Excellent reading skills make it more likely kids will weather personal trauma with their academic credentials intact, since they will be able to keep up with their schoolwork by using only a fraction of their time and emotional energy. In contrast, a personal crisis will usually wipe out a poor reader.

6
Avid reading gives kids a sense of perspective. After seeing life described through the eyes of hundreds of different narrators, they see that there are many ways to look at situations; there are many sides to most issues.

7   Reading helps children to be compassionate. The essence of compassion is the ability to understand another's viewpoint. Reading brings children into thousands of different lives, allowing them to understand these lives in all their complexity. In television sitcoms, problems are solved with a snappy line in a half hour.

8   Avid readers are exposed to a world full of possibilities and opportunities. Maybe they'll read a Michael Crichton thriller and want to become a scientist. Mark Berent's Air Force stories might spark an interest in flying jets. No matter how limited the world in which children live, with reading they can go anywhere. They can dream anything.

9   Avid reading develops critical-thinking skills. Rather than hearing information only in sound bites, avid readers learn to follow complex arguments and remember multifaceted plots.

10 A love of reading is one of the major joys of life. Huddled in a deep chair by the fire with a terrifying thriller; lounging on the beach, laughing at a comic novel; falling asleep over a gentle romance: Without these pleasures, life is a little darker and drabber.

PART I:
99 WAYS TO GET KIDS TO LOVE READING

THE TOP TEN TIPS
(If you read only ten, read these.)

1

Resolve that a love of reading will be your most important educational goal for your children.

Children who hate reading get very little out of even the best schools. They're always behind. They get the reputation of being poor test takers. They start to feel dumb. Pretty soon they get turned off to school altogether.

Kids who love reading, on the other hand, will learn in spite of poor teachers and failing school systems. You can't hold them back, because a love of reading is a love of learning.

A love of reading is the sine qua non of an educated person.

2

Show you value reading rather than tell your children you value it.

Suppose your daughter told you that she really loved her little brother and he *liked* her to take all his Easter candy. He didn't want it anyway! Wouldn't you have a little talk with her about how *saying* something doesn't necessarily make it true?

Saying you value reading doesn't make that true either. You have to show it. So buy books: Have a book-filled house. Go to the library. Spend time yourself reading. Talk about the books that you are enjoying. Engage your children in book discussions. Don't be too busy to do book activities with your children, such as lunch out and a bookstore visit.

And next year put a book into their Easter baskets along with the candy.

3

Don't worry about scheduling time for your children to read. If they love reading, they'll find time.

Kids never have time to clean their rooms and always have time to talk on the phone. Children find time to do the things they love. That's why you need to make sure *reading* is one of the things they love.

4

Don't worry about making your children read only "good" books.

It's very easy for adults who are excellent readers to forget the delight they took in fairly junky reading as children. I remember the blissful ten-year-old happiness I felt upon discovering at my great-aunt's library a cache of Nancy Drew books I hadn't yet read.

Goosebumps and Babysitters Club books are very far from any definition of good literature, and yet these are the books that bring children to a love of reading. In their own good time, children tire of comic books and formula fiction, but by then they'll be reading a little faster and better. *The Horror at Camp Jellyjam* will start to seem a bit fake and silly.

Until then, series books and other formula fiction are wonderful for developing speed and comprehension skills. Kids race through to find out what's going to happen. And they read with the kind of alert, questioning mind-set that is the basis of excellent reading skills. Why are people disappearing from camp? And why are the counselors so . . . odd?

5 Search out books your children will like.

You are going to have to take the initiative in finding reading material for your children. It simply doesn't occur to most children that there are books or magazines on cool things like baseball card collecting or attack reptiles. And, as a practical matter, you're the one with the money and the car.

So be creative and persistent. If your son lives and dies for chess, haunt the hobby and games section of your bookstore. If your daughter spends all her free time kicking around soccer balls, look for anything you can find on soccer.

I've watched teenagers have their first experience with an enthralling book, and it was literally an earthshaking experience for them. They had no *idea* that reading could be so interesting. And after reading that first wonderful book, they are really open to finding another one that is just as good.

Initially loving even just one or two books can expand into a love of reading in general. So find those perfect books!

6

Don't worry that books containing violence will produce violent kids.

Okay: You're watching a movie video, and the monster has just attacked a child. You can close your eyes or fast-forward the film (excellent, parent-preferred ways of reacting)—or you can say, "Wow! Look how high that blood is spurting! And look at those nifty claw marks!" (Not-so-excellent, kid-preferred ways of reacting.)

We can distance—or close out altogether—movie and television violence. But books have narrators. And these narrators are telling the reader how terrified the victim is. And how much pain he's in. In books we can see what's in a victim's mind. And that changes our whole reaction.

While movies can desensitize us to violence, books sensitize us. We're right there, experiencing the horror with the victim. In addition, in horror or suspense books for young people (such as the Goosebumps series), evil is always overcome at the end, usually with the help of courageous children. Rather than making children violent, I think scary books encourage children to be brave and righteous.

Prisons are full of youthful offenders who can barely read. Readers are not the ones who grow up to be violent young adults.

7

Make sure that your children can someday enjoy classics by not pushing them too early.

There's nothing magic about classics. They're older, and so written in a more complex style than most fiction today. Some, like *Pride and Prejudice* by Jane Austen, have heroes and heroines with fine moral sensibilities. Others, like *Madame Bovary* by Gustave Flaubert and *The Great Gatsby* by F. Scott Fitzgerald, have main characters with the moral sense of alley cats.

We would like our children to read classics eventually because of the fine writing style and complex sense of reality in the majority of them. But because of their less-familiar writing styles, they are not books for children just coming to reading. Only kids with fairly sophisticated reading skills can enjoy them.

Sooner or later, if you play your cards right and allow your children to enjoy their series novels and good contemporary fiction, they'll probably work up to classics. But don't try to cram them down their throats too early; they may dislike them so much that they never go back. There's a time for everything.

8

Don't worry if your kids have periods in their lives when they don't avidly read.

It's wonderful if children avidly read all the way through their childhood, and never slow down for their high school or college years. But practically speaking, that probably won't happen. Most kids have times in their lives when other interests or commitments intrude on their reading time. A first love, a particularly demanding academic schedule, or a traumatic event can all cause a temporary halt.

I think it's important that you just wait these times out. Keep magazines around for them to pick up, and occasionally buy them a special new book that just came out. But never nag about their reading slowdown. Treat your children as avid readers who are temporarily between books, so to speak. You want them to keep their love of reading, and their self-image of themselves as *readers*—so they'll go back when they have more time and energy for it.

9

If you have older children who already dislike reading, don't blame yourself.

I've known the most adamant nonreaders who had parents who loved reading and had been brought up in homes filled with books. There can be many reasons for a dislike of reading, ranging from early difficulty in learning how to read, to unfortunate school experiences, to a peer group that disparages readers.

And even if you did do everything wrong—if you never bought books and put all your money instead into huge video systems and cable television in every bedroom—blaming yourself won't accomplish anything. You really loved your children. No one's perfect. Look ahead.

10

Never give up on your children. No matter how old they are, they can be brought to a love of books.

In some ways, it's actually easier to get teenagers and young adults reading. There's more available to read, for one thing—an infinite variety of magazines and books on every conceivable subject. With children, the selection of books and magazines is much more limited.

Plus, older kids have had more time to develop interests. When you find books about their passions, you have almost a 100 percent chance that they'll at least pick them up.

A seventeen-year-old girl who hates to read is usually thought of, in conventional educational terms, as already having missed the boat. But she's only *seventeen*. She has her whole life ahead of her. I'm sure that if you're wily and persistent, sooner or later you'll have the satisfaction of watching her curled up with a fascinating book or magazine, happily reading. And if she keeps reading for pleasure, before too long she'll be an excellent reader who will be able to read and comprehend almost anything.

TIPS FOR PRESCHOOLERS AND BEGINNING READERS

11

Take your children to the library often when they are young and eager to go.

Most little kids love libraries. Yes, they run up and down the handicap ramps, and hide behind the bookcases, but they really enjoy the story hours, and the colorful displays, and the wonderful picture books. Most important, it's pretty easy to find books in libraries that preschoolers will love. They haven't yet gotten to the stage where they want to read only about Michael Jordan.

So take advantage of this early enthusiasm to build a library habit. An avid reading habit requires so many books that it's almost impossible, unless you're independently wealthy, to buy all the books your avid reading children will want. Practically, they have to be ready and willing to go to the library.

So start the library visits now, when they're little. With any luck they'll develop a library habit that will last their whole life. It's much harder to get older children to form the habit of going to the library.

12

Take your children to bookstores as often as you can, and allow them to buy favorite books.

Little kids like to hear favorite books read to them over and over again. And when they start reading they like to read these books over and over again. Having these books permanently on their shelves (or floor) makes them easily available. Plus, for some children, especially children who are very visual, it's important to have books that are fresh and clean, not dingy and worn, as library books can get.

You don't have to buy all your books at regular bookstores. All kinds of stores now carry children's books. While doing errands with your preschoolers at the supermarket or variety store, buy them each a book. It doesn't have to be expensive. Then they'll see that you don't spend money just on milk and bread and spinach and other useless stuff. You regularly spend money on books too.

13 Buy up lots of cheap picture books at garage sales and flea markets.

You can find the most wonderful book bargains, especially at garage sales. Many picture books look almost new, having been through only one or two children. And sometimes they're as cheap as a quarter apiece—or even a dime apiece. Stock up and fill your house. Overflow the bookcases!

It's only when your children are preschoolers that you can count on their loving almost any book you bring home. The more the better! Allow them to cut up the books if they want to. Or smear grape jelly on them. Or build forts with them. Or even read them.

Your motto: You can't have too many books around.

14 Spend more money on books than you spend on Disney videos.

Buy some of the wonderful myth and fairy tale books available. Not only will they help your children love reading, these books will help develop their imaginations.

15 Make read-aloud time fun for your child.

Here are the rules I always followed: First, read whatever books your children want. Yes, they'll choose dumb books. Yes, they'll want the same books read over and over. Yes, sometimes you think you'll SCREAM if you have to read *Goodnight Moon* again. But it's most important that they call the shots here so they know you respect their tastes and they enjoy the reading.

Secondly, ham up the reading. Have fun with it. Mispronounce words on purpose so they can correct you. Use different voices. Giggle together. Make reading a happy, sometimes silly time.

Finally, wrap up the reading quickly when your children's attention lags. Make up the ending you need. "And now Bear is going to have a bath—just like you!"

Enjoyable read-aloud sessions will not only help your children see the wonder and fun of books, these special times will also help them acquire the ability to understand "book" language.

16

Don't read aloud to your children so much that they become too dependent on you for reading entertainment.

Your ultimate goal is not to have children who sit enthralled through read-aloud times. Your ultimate goal is to have children who love reading. So as your children start reading a bit, draw back a little.

Sometimes be too tired to finish the story. "And just then the horrible, creepy, slimy snake started to sneak up behind . . . *yawn* . . . I think I'm getting pretty sleepy. *Yawn. Yawn.* Why don't you go off to bed—you can take the book with you if you want—because I'm having trouble keeping my eyes . . . *ZZZzzzzz.*"

You do this so that your children become independent readers—and also to prevent them from becoming whiny, clingy, read-to-me-all-the-time kind of kids. No one likes kids to behave like that.

17

Help your preschoolers plan play activities that involve books.

Encourage your young children to "read" bedtime stories to their dolls. Or to play bookstore or library. Or to dress up and act out the activities of their favorite characters.

You want to do this to make books a part of their daily lives, but also to give them opportunities to do reading-type activities with their friends.

18

When your children seem ready, play some beginning reading games.

The rule here is that the games have to be fun for your child. That's why it's better for you to make up games than to depend on workbooks or canned programs, which all seem to have a built-in dullness factor. If you're making up the games, you can change them at a moment's notice.

What do I mean by games? Easy

things, like guessing with your daughter what letter foods for lunch start with. "Let's see, you want a ssssssandwich. Hmmm. That's a hard one. Does it start with the letter M?" Let her giggle and correct you. Or let her quiz you about what letter things start with. Remember, kids love being in control, and they *especially* love being in control of their parents.

You can also make up easy, short shopping lists, and let her cross out each item as you get it. Or let her say her favorite word when you're reading a story to her and you come to it. Or let her paste name tags on household items, like the couch or her little brother. Any activity that makes her more familiar with reading is good, *as long as she is enjoying it.*

19 Don't get hung up on the whole-language-versus-phonics debate.

What is this great debate? Briefly, phonics advocates believe that early instruction in reading should be all phonics based. Children should be taught how to sound out words they don't know. This kind of teaching leads to reading lists of similar-sounding words, as well as early stories that are written more to highlight a particular phonics skill than to delight children with a wonderful story.

Whole-language advocates think that children learn in a more global way, perhaps with some phonics drills but mostly by being immersed in interesting stories. Kids learn to recognize some words by sight, or by guessing from the pictures, rather than by sounding everything out.

I think a combination of methods is probably best, because some children learn best through auditory means—they do well with phonics—while some kids are more visual, and so do better with sight words or guessing from pictures. Some lucky children seem to learn easily any way.

20 Be aware of how your children learn best.

This is another reason you should do a little reading instruction yourself with your children. Then you can check out the lay of the land. If your son, for example, never remembers more than one thing at a time that you tell him, or is still using the wrong forms for words long after his playmates ("throwed" instead of "threw"), you might want to emphasize visual games, like making name tags, or playing Reading Fish, where you match words instead of objects.

On the other hand, if you have a daughter who is always singing little songs, with all the correct lyrics, or mimicking her grandmother's voice, you can try some easy phonics games. With any luck, you can have your children far enough along in reading before first grade that it won't matter what kind of instruction their school uses.

You want to do this because children tend to love activities they're good at.

You want your children to be the good readers in their school.

21

If your child doesn't enjoy beginning reading activities, back off. It may be too early.

Some children are just a little slower to acquire all the processing abilities that make learning to read easy. And this shouldn't be a big deal. We're all a little slow in some areas of life. I still can never remember where I've parked.

So if your son would much rather be out in the mud, working along with his buddies digging a tunnel to China, relax and let him. Just keep getting him interesting books about earth-moving equipment, and China, and how things are made. Keep reading to him. Sooner or later it will all come together.

22

Read easy comic books to your children.

I did this with my children only because they insisted. "You want me to read a Richie Rich comic again?" I'd groan, going against all my own advice. "*Another* one?" They'd nod confidently and happily, and I'd reluctantly begin.

But here's what happened. Pretty soon they'd be willing to read the part of a really minor character. And then a character with a few more lines. And finally, they were reading all the good parts, and I just got to be the maid and the butler. Very soon after that they were reading the whole comic themselves.

I think the comics were so good, because my children are pretty visual, and with the pictures they could usually figure out the words they didn't know. They all loved Richie Rich comics, and read them for years. We still have them in boxes, taking up all our closet space.

23

Be really enthusiastic about your children's early attempts at reading.

Doing new, difficult tasks is always hard. Praise really helps.

So tell your children how wonderful they are when they start reading. You love hearing them read! And tell them immediately how to pronounce any word they ask you about, but never be so tactless as to mention the 50 percent of the words they don't know they are pronouncing wrong.

Focus on what they're doing *right*. They're reading!

24

When your children start reading, buy them really easy books and comics.

It's tempting when children start reading to buy books a little too difficult for them so they can "reach" and learn more. But too often this discourages kids. You want reading to be fun, so buy them books they can zip through with little effort. Then they'll feel like terrific readers.

In your house they *are* terrific readers! Right?

25 If they request a book that you know is too difficult, buy it for them anyway.

I'm always amazed at what children can read if they are interested enough. It may take them hours to read just a few pages. They may have to sound out every other word as they go along. But it's wonderful what children can read *when they really want to.*

Sometimes children will read a little bit of a book, decide it's too hard, put it away, and then try again in a few months. I've known children who have taken years to get through a book. That's fine. As long as they are loving the book, leave them alone.

26

Don't worry if your children love picture books long after their friends have started reading chapter books.

Very visual kids are often slow to come to books that have nothing but boring black print. That's okay. There are wonderful picture books available. You can let them have their fill without worrying that at the age of seventeen they'll still be lugging home Richard Scarry's *Best Word Book Ever* from the library.

And even after they have gradually moved to chapter books with no pictures, you should keep an eye out for more-advanced books that are also illustrated. Very visual kids are at risk of never becoming avid readers, so you need to do anything you can to help them find reading pleasurable.

27

After your children are reading well themselves, continue reading to them, or let them read to you.

You don't want your children to think that the cozy, friendly one-on-one parent time is over once they start reading. Plus, by still having read-aloud times you can introduce your children to new authors and help them get accustomed to language that may still be too sophisticated for them to read themselves.

And by encouraging them to read to you, you are identifying them as special, literate members of your family.

28

Don't choose a nursery school simply because it teaches children to read.

I think the main criteria for nursery schools should be that they are warm, happy, relaxed places for children. If the school can teach a little beginning reading too, that's fine, but not necessary.

The last thing you want is a high-pressured school that tries to make children read before they are ready. Then not only will they hate school, they'll hate reading too.

TIPS FOR ELEMENTARY-SCHOOL CHILDREN

29

Encourage the reading of series books such as the American Girl books or Goosebumps.

When kids fall in love with a series, it's always easy to find their next book. And if they've loved one book in the series, they will most likely love them all.

Kids tear through series, picking up speed and vocabulary. By the time they've finished the series, they're reading a little better, and have begun to form the habit of reading.

30 **Recognize that avid readers tend to "binge" read.**

When kids are enjoying a specific series or books by a certain author, they won't want to read anything else until they've read every book. That's okay! They're doing a lot of reading. And sooner or later they'll move on.

31 **Continue to encourage library use, but recognize that many of the books your children will want (such as the next book in a beloved series) may not be available in a library and will have to be bought.**

Unfortunately, with budget cuts and generally low funding, libraries often may not have a certain book right at the time your child desperately wants to read it. If you can manage it at all, buy that book for your child.

32 **Be careful that you don't schedule so many activities for your children that they have little time to read.**

Between soccer leagues and skiing lessons and piano practice, many elementary-school-age children lead frantic lives. There's no need for this. They have their whole lives to learn how to ski.

Be sure your children have lots of unscheduled time so they can read when they want to. Don't think they're wasting their time if they spend Saturday morning lying on their beds, sorting and reading their X-men comics, instead of playing baseball. True, children may learn teamwork and how to deal with adversity while playing a sport. But kids don't have to love sports to learn these valuable skills. Kids *have* to read to acquire sophisticated literacy skills. There's no other way.

33

Spend as much on books and magazines for your children as you spend on other entertainment and sports activities for them.

What message are you sending your daughter if you spend hundreds of dollars on soccer equipment, club fees, and summer camp, but refuse to subscribe to *Seventeen* magazine or *Soccer America*?

Just think how many paperbacks you could buy for your son if you spend the same amount of money on books that you spend on his hockey pads and skates, fees, ice time, and travel expenses.

34

Recognize that very athletic children tend to be at higher risk for failing to develop a reading habit.

So be innovative. Donate magazine subscriptions to your child's team so that reading material will be around for road trips. Ask the coach to support reading efforts. Find books and articles about teams your child especially loves. Open the newspaper to the sports page at breakfast.

35 Encourage the development of hobbies such as coin or doll or sports-card collecting.

Kids can become really fanatic about hobbies. What's good about this is that then they'll read everything they can find on the subject. And luckily there are magazines and books on almost any subject imaginable.

36 Many children love reading plays aloud.

Libraries usually have a good selection of plays for children. Read them yourself with your kids, or help them arrange play-reading parties with their friends.

You might even try reading aloud books in parts, especially books that have a good deal of dialogue. Let your child be the main character, and you read the narrator parts, and the parts of the lesser characters. This can be a lot of fun, especially with a comic novel.

37 Allow only one video during sleep-overs, and have plenty of magazines and comics available.

This comes under the reading-with-friends category. You want to do what you can to get your children's friends reading. As kids get older, their friends gain more and more influence over them. Having friends who love reading makes it more likely your children will keep reading.

I used to leave the magazines and comics out, and then say sternly (after the video and the snacks and the mandatory pillow fight and the games and the gossip), "Now I want everyone *to go to sleep! I want it quiet! I want everyone lying down!*" I'd stand with my arms folded, looking threatening, until all were in their sleeping bags. Then I'd fade away, and they'd grab the magazines and comics.

38 Don't worry when your children exhibit some quirky reading habits.

I'm starting to think that few avid readers pick up one book, read it through, put it down, and then pick up another, all the while sitting in some normal reading position. I find that avid readers often skip around in books, sometimes skipping endings altogether. Others have to eat or squirm around while they read. Kids bend book pages, hum and listen to a Walkman, or even watch television, while reading. Many jump from book to book, sometimes finishing earlier books, sometimes not. They'll want to read nothing but a horror author for months, and then decide they're never reading that author again.

But none of that matters. They're reading!

39

If your kids attend summer camp, send them off with piles of reading material as well as including favorite magazines and comics with your weekly letters to them.

Few camps allow much television watching, and almost all camps have afternoon rest time. This is the perfect situation for reading.

Your children will probably end up supplying their whole cabin with magazines and paperbacks, but that's fine. They'll be seen as the literate ones, the ones who know what's good to read.

Just don't count on ever getting any of this reading material back. It will disappear, along with your children's only pair of good shoes, all their socks, and their expensive new sleeping bags. Poof! Gone!

READING-FRIENDLY ROUTINES AND HOUSES

40

When you're looking for a new house, try to find one with a big shady front porch that you can furnish with a swing, rocking chairs, and a table for books.

Kids love to hang out on porches, watching the world go by, seeing and being seen by friends—and reading! Front porches have been producing readers for generations.

41

Houses without porches can still have friendly reading spots on decks or patios, in tree houses, or indoors in special reading corners.

Children seem to love special little places where they can curl up away from the world. Just provide reading material for these spots.

42

Try to live within walking or biking distance of a library.

This encourages children to become independent in selecting and bringing home their own books.

43

Plan special rituals around book buying.

For example, before you go on vacation every year, make the day before you leave a special visit-the-bookstore day. Or be sure to bring your children to a newsstand before getting on an airplane, so they can stock up on magazines. Buy a special Christmas book for your children every December, or a special summer book at the end of the school year in June.

What you want is for book buying and reading to be woven into the fabric of your children's lives. On special occasions—birthdays, holidays, or vacations—get them thinking about reading.

44

Look in specialty stores for reading material about your children's favorite activities.

Hobby stores, music stores, and sports stores often carry a large selection of specialized reading material. This is a great boon because these are stores your children are likely to love to hang out in. Help them get in the habit of checking out the magazine and book racks as well as the clothes, CD, or model sections.

45

It's especially important that fathers spend time reading to boys and helping them find books.

In our culture, reading isn't seen as tough and hard-hitting an activity as playing a sport, or fixing a car, or camping or hunting. A father needs to spend a good deal of time doing reading activities with his son so that his son sees that reading, also, is a cool, masculine thing to do.

Again and again, in conversations with my avid-reading high-school boys, I notice they mention how their fathers helped get them reading.

46 **Keep magazines, books, and comics in the kitchen for reading during informal meals and snacks.**

You want to establish that all-important reading-food connection.

47 **Realize that reading is messier than watching television.**

Nothing that children do is as tidy as watching television. You have chair and child in the room, and most of the time the child doesn't even move off the chair. Reading doesn't work like that.

Readers tend to leave books and magazines and newspapers scattered everywhere—on the kitchen table, on the floor of the living room, all over bedrooms, even on the porch and in the car. You can demand that your readers return everything to neatly designated shelves, but children may find that that's more trouble than it's worth. After a while they'll start thinking, Who needs that hassle? I'm just going to turn on the television. Programs, after all, don't spill out and need to be straightened up afterward.

I think demanding absolute neatness with books is too great a risk. It's better to tolerate a little mess if you can.

48 Keep a supply of magazines, comics, and short books in the car.

With soccer practice, skiing lessons, and after-school activities, not to mention family outings, we all spend much too much of our time in cars. Perhaps you can set things up so your children do a bit a reading there. I've found comics and magazines work the best.

Plus, kids absorbed in reading are also much less likely to fight or whine.

49

Bring reading material with you when taking children out to eat in restaurants.

You have your kids trapped, sitting down, waiting for food. They could sprinkle salt all over the table, or kick their chairs . . . or read!

Later, when they get older, you can work on social conversation and polite dinner table demeanor.

50

Take long train trips with your children and remember to bring along lots of reading material.

While some children get motion sickness from reading in a car, almost everyone can read comfortably in a train. So buy them a cozy snack and bring out the magazines and paperbacks.

51

Give bookstore gift certificates as presents to your children's friends.

This comes under the heading of developing reading friends.

I'd attach these as little extras to birthday presents, since, if they were the main gift, your children might get a reputation for being lousy gift givers.

Another good thing about gift certificates is that it gets the parents of your children's friends into bookstores too. Maybe they'll be pleased to see their children excited about books. Maybe they'll bring their kids back and spend some of their own money on books.

52

Encourage your children to lend their books to friends.

Of course the books will permanently disappear but, again, reading friends are invaluable—much better than television-watching friends.

53

Return your children's overdue library books.

Don't nag; just return them yourself, or your kids will stop wanting to go to the library. They can learn responsibility by taking out the trash or feeding the dog.

54

Don't worry if your children don't immediately read the material you bring home.

They may read it later. Many times children put books up on the shelf in their rooms, and then months or even years later, pick them up.

Kids will sometimes read a small part of a book and then finish it much later. Or they may read the whole book and never bother to mention to you that they did.

Even if they never do read the book, at least they know you value reading and are willing to spend money on books for them. That's no little thing.

55

Don't give your children a lights-out time at night. Let them read as long as they want to.

You want your children to form the unbreakable habit of reading themselves to sleep. Then, no matter how busy they are, or what else is happening in their lives, they'll do at least a little reading every day.

DEALING WITH TV AND COMPUTERS

56

Have as few televisions in the house as possible, preferably no more than one.

With many televisions you risk always having a television available when your children want one. Then they are never forced to look elsewhere for entertainment.

Without a television they will almost

certainly turn to books for stories and excitement. Even if you have just one television, they will often turn to reading since other members of the family will frequently watch programs they don't like, and they'll have to find something else to do.

57 Resist getting cable.

Cable television simply has too many enticing programs for children—endless cartoons, movies, sitcom reruns. There's a good chance that on a slow, boring afternoon, nothing will be on regular television that your children enjoy. But with cable there's always *something* that kids will watch.

Plus, cable is expensive. Use that money to buy reading material.

I'd consider cable only if I had avid readers already, or if my husband loved sports, say, and my children hated sports. Then I'd get a sports channel in the hope that he'd usurp the television every night. But I'd never get a movie channel or a children's channel. You can always rent videos for that special movie or children's show.

58 Never allow children to have televisions in their bedrooms.

Never, never, never! It's hard to think of a worse thing to do, reading-wise. Children will fall asleep with the television instead of a juicy book. As teenagers' lives become more frantic, bedtime is often the only time they do any pleasure reading.

I also think a bedroom television causes children to be more isolated. They are always going to their room, shutting the door, and watching heaven knows what. A book is more mobile. They may hide up in their room reading, but they're also likely to read in family areas, such as the kitchen or patio or den or front porch.

If you already have a television in your child's room, get it out somehow.

59

Don't make the television room in your house too inviting.

Books don't need the competition of soft couches, plush carpeting, or a large screen TV. How about a room with a small black and white set, folding chairs, and little heat?

It's the other rooms, the rooms full of books, that you want your kids to hang out in. Make sure these are the rooms with the comfortable chairs, the sunny window seats, the sofas to sprawl on. Otherwise you risk having your children crash in front of the television simply because it's in the most comfortable room in the house.

60

If your children are watching lots of television and doing little reading, consider really restricting television, or banning it altogether.

There's always a risk in micromanaging your children's lives in such a way that they are very different from their friends. And raising children without any television, or with very little television, does set them apart. It's a risk.

But I think you have to balance this with the greater risk of raising children who never read for pleasure. If children never read for pleasure, they will never be accomplished readers. Reading will always be a painful chore rather than a source of fun. You are ensuring that they will never be top performers in any field that requires reading—which is any professional, business, or academic field. You are ensuring that the farther along they go in school, the more trouble they will have. In our information-rich age, you are really consigning them to second-class-citizen status.

I think that's a much bigger risk.

61 Don't feel you need to provide computers for your children.

Educational gurus who are touting technology as the answer to the education crisis are, quite simply, wrong. *Books* are the answer. Yes, the workforce of the future will need to use computers, but avid-reading children acquire computer skills very easily. Since they read so well, they can follow complicated instruction books. With their writing skills, they quickly fall in love with e-mail, and flood all their acquaintances with endless messages.

Poor readers haven't learned to process information efficiently enough to have a lot of success with computers. Plus, playing endless computer games often takes up the time they should be spending reading.

62 If you keep in mind the pitfalls, a computer can help your children be more literate.

There are fun reading games and wonderful picture books on CD-ROMs that may motivate a young child to begin reading. For older children there are interesting educational sites on the Internet as well as huge online bookstores available for browsing.

I think the rule of thumb should be

this: If your children are already avid readers, I wouldn't worry about turning them loose with computers. If they rarely read for pleasure, I'd keep as much interesting reading material and as few other distractions (like computers) around as I could. Reading has to come first.

KIDS WITH A READING DISABILITY

63

If your child is very late in learning how to read, arrange for learning disability testing.

Most children acquire beginning reading skills by second grade, or certainly by third. If you have a seven- or eight-year-old who is reading very poorly, or not at all, have the child's auditory and visual processes tested. Some children, for example, have perfect hearing but don't process what they hear very well. Perhaps they can't easily tell the difference between similar sounds (auditory discrimination), or remember what they hear (auditory memory). You can require your school to do this testing, or have it done privately.

You're trying to find out if your child has some deficit that is making learning to read harder. For example, if you have a daughter with a very poor visual memory, she'll need to be taught reading by oral means, with phonics. Most children are a little stronger in some areas than in others but can really learn in many ways. But some children are so weak in a processing area that they require specialized teaching that utilizes their areas of strength.

Look at it this way. If you had a son with a severe hearing loss, you wouldn't give him elaborate oral directions on how to get somewhere. You'd show him a map. Likewise, a child with very poor auditory discrimination is going to have a hard time learning to read with phonics instruction. He doesn't *hear* the differences in sounds.

64

Children diagnosed as having ADD (attention deficit disorder) or ADHD (attention deficit hyperactivity disorder) can also become excellent readers.

I know that conventional wisdom suggests that these children can't sit still long enough, or can't concentrate well enough, ever to become avid readers. But I haven't found this to be the case. The key is linking these children to material they are wildly curious to read.

Start out with short material such as comics, magazines, or Choose Your Own Adventure books. Then gradually give them longer works of equally high interest. The interesting thing you'll notice is that many of these children hyperactively read once they find a book they love. They sit absolutely motionless and hunch over the book with complete concentration. Bombs could go off around them. It's so amazing to see, because usually, of course, a fly that happens to cruise over their desk distracts them from their work for the next ten minutes. But if that book is *really* good . . .

Find this interesting reading material for your child at home, and suggest to his teacher that maybe if she lets him read *Monster Blood* instead of insisting he read *The Bridge to Terabithia,* he might settle down and become a productive class member.

For an ADD child I'd also search out the best professional help I could find. Sometimes medication or other therapies really help.

65 Older children and teenagers who read well below grade level should also be tested.

Often, older children have learned to compensate for a learning disability themselves. If they have a good auditory memory and a poor visual memory, for example, they may find themselves listening hard in class but not taking many notes. But if the processing deficit is severe enough, they may not have been able to compensate and may be very behind in reading—which ensures that they will be behind in all their subjects.

So arrange for testing to see what the situation is.

66 If a learning disability is diagnosed, insist on specialized instruction.

Public Law 94–142 (a federal law) requires states to provide special education services for children with disabilities, and this includes learning disabilities. School districts are required by law to write up and implement an individualized learning plan, after it has been approved by the child's parents or guardian. As a parent, you have a lot of legal clout.

The law also mandates that children be "mainstreamed" (placed in regular classes) if possible. This means that unless your child has such severe disabilities that a regular classroom situation isn't possible, he should be in a regular class but should receive specialized instruction in reading.

Let's say your son has a very poor auditory memory. If his auditory discrimination is okay, he can probably benefit from some phonics instruction, but most of his reading instruction should be visual and kinesthetic—writing letters out, playing games with flash cards, and the like.

His teacher should be alerted that he will have trouble remembering oral instruction and oral directions. Things need to be written, or drawn on the board, for him. Your son should also be coached in ways of compensating for his poor auditory memory.

67 A child with a disability needs more parental help in developing a love of reading.

A reading disability means that your child is starting behind most of his classmates. This in itself will make reading less attractive to him. In addition, he will need more direct instruction to learn how to read, and most kids think direct instruction is a drag.

In addition to that, many kids hate being pulled out of class to receive this direct instruction. They feel stigmatized.

You're going to have to be very sensitive to all of this. You'll be tempted to let him use his home time to do things he likes doing, and does well, to build up his self-confidence. But you need to get him doing reading things.

A boy with poor coordination will have a much harder time learning to play tennis, but with a lot of practice he can play a respectable game. Likewise, a child with a learning disability can become a good reader, but he'll need a great deal of practice.

So you need to pull out all the stops and try to get your son to love reading—so he'll practice.

68 Buy reading material with lots of pictures for children with auditory processing disabilities.

Comic books are pure gold for children with poor auditory discrimination or a poor auditory memory. They can figure out the words from the pictures, and the riveting, adventure-filled stories keep them interested and help them like reading.

I would also get plenty of magazines, and even picture books, as long as your child is willing to read them.

69 Make sure your children with poor visual memories are taught to read phonetically.

Kids with poor visual memories or poor visual discrimination usually can't learn to read by flash cards or other sight-recognition methods. They simply don't retain the image of the word for very long in their memories. Phonics is your only hope with these children.

The good news is that these kids, if taught correctly, often become excellent readers because once they learn to read they don't need a great visual memory. They'll never spell well—and don't ever expect them to pass a map

test in history—but they are often terrific, avid readers.

70

Emphasize frequently to your reading disabled child that slowness in learning to read has nothing to do with intelligence.

Reading disabled children really need to be reassured. They'll probably be put in a low-level reading group; they'll have a tutor helping them; they'll watch their friends race through books that they still can't read at all.

Use analogies with them. If your daughter is a very good artist, explain that she has a special artistic talent. Many kids don't have this talent, but that doesn't make them dumb. Other kids have more "reading talent" than she does, but that doesn't make them smarter than she is. It just means they can learn to read a little more quickly.

But always emphasize that she can be a very good reader too; she needs to practice.

71

Keep a close eye on how reading is taught in your child's school.

A very good, avid reader can survive a year or two of teachers who do little reading or who insist their students read books they don't like. But a year or two like this can put a learning disabled child permanently behind.

So if your child is in a shaky reading situation, you should probably get active. Explain to the teacher that your child isn't dumb; he just does much better in reading if he can read books that he likes and that aren't too difficult for him. Offer to supply the books. Offer to help the teacher in any way you can to make the situation better for your child.

And remember that you always have the legal clout of the special education law behind you. The school is required to provide an "appropriate" education.

72

You really need to keep long-term reading goals in mind with learning disabled children.

It's very tempting to try to do anything just to get these children through their classes. If your daughter can't read a class-assigned book, for example, her teacher may arrange for her to listen to the book on tape. Or she may be given a special education tutor to walk her through it.

But I think these stop-gap measures defeat your long-term goal, which is to make your daughter a competent reader who can function well in any job. To get there, she has to *read*—not listen to tapes or a tutor's summary.

73

As much as possible, let your child make the decisions about what special education services to receive.

When children make the decision for tutoring help, they are much more likely to make good use of it. If your child wants to cancel all help—particularly if this is an older child or a teenager—you should probably go along with the decision, at least for a while. Sometimes children feel so stigmatized by having to go to a learning center that any benefit is outweighed by their anger.

And sooner or later your child will have to learn to work independently anyway. If you've managed to develop the child as a reader, he'll probably be all right.

WHICH BOOKS FOR WHICH KIDS?

Note: In this section I will be referring to different types of readers. For specific reading suggestions, check the lists at the end of this book. For a more complete description of reading pathways, check my book *Keeping Kids Reading*.

74

Pay attention to your children's developing reading tastes.

Generally some children, mostly boys, like books with good-versus-evil themes, while others, usually girls, like books about interpersonal relationships. So boys tend to like adventure stories filled with good guys and bad guys, while girls tend to like books about friendships or family problems or young love.

75

Children also usually have a preference for realistic or imaginative fiction.

Kids who like realistic fiction usually enjoy mysteries or espionage, or believable relationship books. Children whose tastes run to more imaginative books prefer fantasy, science fiction, or books with magic or occult elements.

76

If you have a daughter who loves pretending and playing with dolls and stuffed animals, look for books with imaginative or magic elements.

Generally these girls are drawn to books that have dolls that come alive, or witches or other interesting (but not scary) characters who do magic. Often, too, they much prefer happy endings. Sometimes they like books set in the past, particularly if there is a rosy glow of nostalgia (such as in the Betsy-Tacy books). On the whole they like books that give them a short, harmless escape from reality.

77

If your daughter is more down-to-earth and is very caught up with the dynamics of her social group, look for books set in the present that depict relationships more realistically.

Generally these girls like to read books to find out about things. They'll read a series like the Babysitters Club books to find how friends should act with each other, or high school romances to get a head start on understanding how high school works. Novels about children with problems are usually of interest to this group also. Generally they read for information.

78 If you have a son who is imaginative and loves good-versus-evil adventures, try fantasy or science fiction.

Boys like this sometimes seem to be in their own world. As young children they do much imaginative play, often with dragons or swords. They often daydream in school, especially in elementary school. They can be very frustrating because they seem so bright but often don't do well in school.

The good news is that if they fall in love with reading through their fantasy and science fiction interests, they often go on to become excellent students. When they decide to settle down and work, their sophisticated reading skills and wide frames of reference ensure that they get top grades without a whole lot of effort.

79

If you have a child who doesn't see much sense in fantasy, but likes good-versus-evil themes, try adventure stories with realistic settings, or nonfiction.

This type of reader is generally a very practical, down-to-earth boy. He might like fishing or camping or sports. He often works hard in school but is at great risk of not gaining sophisticated reading skills since the kinds of books he can easily like—survival, war, or sports stories—are in short supply in most elementary schools. Parents need to make a special effort to find interesting reading for this kind of child. If you can just keep him reading enough in elementary school to get him up to a respectable reading level, he can find many adult authors to read in junior high and high school (such as Clive Cussler and Michael Crichton).

80

Any book whose plot involves your child's special interest is a good bet.

If your daughter likes horseback riding, you're lucky. There are literally hundreds of children's books about horseback riding.

Unfortunately, there is no other interest that is so well represented in children's fiction. But there are some baseball and football books, some books about hunting and camping, and even some books recently about gymnastics and swimming. If you can't find books on these subjects, at least look for magazines. There are magazines about everything, from coin collecting to snowboarding.

81

Almost all children like humorous books.

Even kids who say they don't like any kind of books at all can usually be enticed into trying a book that is funny. For that adamant nonreader, start with collections of Sunday comics such as

Garfield or *The Far Side*, or writers like Roald Dahl (for young readers) or Robert B. Parker (for older readers), or even joke books.

Any reading they do should sooner or later lead them to other books.

82 It's important that children read about some characters they can identify with.

If your children want to learn more about their ethnic heritage, or have some special problem, try to find books that have characters similar to them. For children to love reading, it's very important that they see themselves in books.

A book or character that illuminates a child's own experience ties that child to books forever.

83

Don't be surprised if your children seem to change reading tastes.

As children get older, their tastes expand. A friend might suggest a Stephen King book to your daughter, who has read only relationship books. She might find that his books have enough relationship elements in them to pull her through, and she might, at the same time, develop a taste for more action.

Boys, on the other hand, as they get older, sometimes develop a little curiosity about, and an appreciation of, books that highlight relationships.

So always be alert to new types of books that your kids might enjoy.

SCHOOL TIPS

84

Look for schools that allow their students wide choice in reading material.

Probably the worst thing that can happen to children with regard to reading is being forced to read books that are of little interest to them.

Kids usually enter school feeling friendly toward books and reading. But when they are made to read books they see little sense in and are told that the books they like aren't good enough for school reading, they soon lose interest in reading altogether.

Personally, I think kids should be given a wide selection of reading material all the way up through high school. If your children's school doesn't allow students much choice—and most schools don't—I don't have any easy solutions for you. I can tell you that children who are avid readers already are much less harmed by inflexible reading policies, since they can enjoyably read almost any book. But poor readers can't, and will be further turned off to reading.

If you can figure out a way to get schools to shift their emphasis from teacher-assigned reading to student-choice reading, please let me know.

85 **Look for schools that give kids time to read in class.**

Teachers can say to students, "Sit down now and quietly read," and kids will do it. It's harder for parents to be that directive. A quiet reading period in school can go a long way toward helping children develop a love and habit of reading.

Plus, when kids read in school, they see their friends and teachers also reading—which tends to make reading a more desirable activity. They'll want to try the same books their friends are reading; they'll start lending books to each other and trading books. With any luck, a real reading community will de-

velop—an invaluable support for readers of any age.

Many elementary schools do allow
for a little free reading time in class,
and the practice is well respected
enough that I think you can question
schools that don't do it.

86 Look for schools that use little or no ability grouping, especially with reading.

There are many problems with tracking
students, but a major one is that when
most of the students in a class have the
same reading level, it's almost irre-
sistible for the teacher to require that
everyone read the same book. There is
little incentive for offering independent
reading options.

In addition, if your child is put into a
low-level reading group, he may well
start to hate reading altogether. People
don't like to do things that make them
feel incompetent or dumb.

So look for schools where kids of
various levels of reading ability are

grouped together and then allowed to read at their own pace. Slower-reading children are motivated by seeing the interesting books their classmates are reading. Avid-reading children aren't held back, but can also occasionally read an old, easy favorite without getting behind.

87 Look for schools with large classroom libraries as well as a good school library staffed by a professional librarian.

Children need to have lots of books right in school with them, so the librarian, teachers, and friends can help with book selection. A good school librarian, especially, is invaluable in steering kids to books they'll like.

Having many books throughout a school also sends the message that this school values reading, and that its staff understands that kids need to love reading, and do lots of reading, to become good readers.

88

Look for schools with many other activities in addition to sports.

Sports are wonderful for children, but other activities tend to lead them more in the direction of books. A good school newspaper can encourage children to write book reviews and do research for articles. A drama club encourages play reading. French or Spanish clubs encourage reading in other languages. Debate and speech clubs require reading about current events. Poetry clubs, literary magazines, and even fun events like limerick contests can all help children develop into literate adults.

89

Don't pressure your children to be perfect students.

Pressure to get A's on all assignments drives out pleasure reading. Children are afraid to take time to enjoy a book. They feel like they always have to be doing one more bit of homework.

After a while, perfectionist children

don't even achieve well because they can't relax enough to come up with creative insights.

90 Don't force your children to read an assigned book that they hate.

If your kids are willing to read required, hated books on their own, fine. Stand aside and cheer. But parents shouldn't align themselves with a school curriculum that seems designed to make kids hate reading. Give your children any help they ask for, and keep doing home things to help them love reading. But don't exert pressure to make your children do tedious, too-difficult school reading. Let the decision to read or not read be theirs.

I know that this advice flies in the face of conventional wisdom, but I think few people realize how destructive it is for children to be forced to read material they hate. If your children keep getting these kinds of assignments, all your choices are bad. But I think your least harmful choice, in the long run, is to refuse to force your children to do this kind of reading.

Look at it this way: Children who love reading, and read all the time, will do well academically in spite of an occasional bad grade gotten for not doing required reading. And children who hate reading will never read well enough to do really well academically, no matter how much pressure you put on them. The *only* chance kids have to be well-educated adults is to develop a love and habit of reading. Make *that* be your priority, not a high grade on homework in the fifth grade.

91 Don't give children extensive help with long, complicated reading reports.

Some children are assigned book reports that are so detailed and involved, that doing them makes them hate a book they originally liked.

I don't think you should help your children with these. Let them handle them however they will. If they choose not to do them, or do them in a sloppy fashion, perhaps the teacher will see that that assignment isn't working well. If they do a great job on them, well, perhaps they really don't mind them.

But if you help your children do well on assignments they really hate, the teacher will never see how inappropriate that assignment was. And she'll keep giving more assignments like it.

92 Publicly praise teachers who are trying to run classrooms that nurture readers.

Teachers are often afraid to do such reading-friendly activities as allowing students a good deal of free reading time in their classes. So support these teachers. Write letters of praise to their principals and school committees. Thank them for what they are doing. Offer to donate books to their classroom libraries.

When other teachers hear of this

community support, they may find the courage to do some reading-friendly activities themselves.

TIPS FOR TEENAGERS

93 **Try to move your teenagers to adult authors.**

Many children, girls especially, who avidly read as children never make the jump to adult authors. Oh, they read the adult authors assigned in their school courses, but never think to go looking for books on their own. Often these are kids who did a great deal of reading when they were younger. But then school became more demanding, activities became more important, and the authors they used to love started seeming childish. In their new busy teenage lives, pleasure reading was the thing to go.

So be very conscious of making sure your teenagers start discovering adult authors. And I wouldn't be too worried about girls who start reading steamy love books or boys who prefer novels full of mayhem and warfare. My rule of thumb, developed after twenty-six years of teaching high school, is this: Teenagers who *read* about sex and violence are less likely to engage in it. I think they start to see that actions have consequences—promiscuous heroines rarely end up well—or else they simply have their curiosity assuaged, and so are less likely to experiment. At any rate, avid readers are the students with a future, and this awareness itself prevents much teenage self-destructive behavior.

94 Look for adult authors who write the kind of books your teenager enjoyed when younger.

If your daughter loved books about families and relationships, introduce her to authors like Rosamunde Pilcher and Maeve Binchy. She probably won't like writers of technothrillers, like Tom Clancy.

If your son, on the other hand, loved the survival books of Gary Paulsen, you might try a writer like Clive Cussler, who writes survival/adventure-type books. But I wouldn't suggest a writer like Danielle Steel. Even as your children get more sophisticated, their sensibilities remain remarkably the same.

95 **When teenagers start driving, send them on errands that take them to bookstores and newsstands. Mention that you'll repay them (up to whatever amount you can afford) for any money they spend on reading material.**

It doesn't occur to most teenagers to walk into a bookstore on their own, or to buy books. You want to change this mind-set by whatever means you can. It's the kids who hang around bookstores who are usually the best readers.

Otherwise, they'll spend all their time in video stores and pizza parlors.

96

Keep an eye on your teenager's schedule.

Although I really think kids make time for activities they love doing, some teenagers pack their schedule so full with sports and after-school jobs that they really have no time for almost anything else but eating and sleeping. Their schoolwork suffers, and pleasure reading usually disappears completely.

Is it really that necessary that your teenager work? Remember, lousy college board scores will hurt your son more when it comes to college acceptance than the spending money he gets from a minimum-wage job will help him.

97

Be sympathetic when teenagers are experiencing some of the frequent ups and downs of teenage life, but also provide books that suggest ways of dealing with their issues.

While we're always sorry to see our children unhappy, we don't want to overlook an interest that might get them reading. And they may accept sensible advice from an author that they won't accept from us.

98

If your teenager plays a sport, be sure to subscribe to any local papers that provide sports coverage.

Most local papers are very good about covering high school sports. When kids realize their sports exploits are actually written up in black and white for everyone to read, you can't keep the newspaper from them.

With any luck, after a while they'll read more than just the sports.

FINALLY

99

Keep a perspective. Top reading skills should be your most important *educational* goal but not your most important life goal for your children.

We want children who are compassionate, hardworking people of integrity. We want them to laugh readily and to find pleasure in life's daily activities. We want them to be loyal to friends, and to be able to form loving family relationships. If they are also readers, they'll have an easier time in school and have many more opportunities available to them. But they won't necessarily have better lives.

Encourage reading, but never lose sight of the qualities that are even more important.

PART II: 100 BOOKS THEY'LL LOVE

NOTE

I tried to divide these lists into useful categories, according to children's likes and dislikes. For most children you can probably pull books from more than one list. You might, for example, have a son who loves horror books but who also loves baseball.

I omitted nonfiction books, magazines, and comic books only for lack of space, and because they're generally easier to find. Nonfiction books on hunting are all in one section of a bookstore or library, while fiction books about hunting are usually shelved alphabetically by author with all the other fiction. But do keep nonfiction, magazines, and comics in mind when choosing books, especially if you're looking for books for kids who dislike reading.

There are many, *many* other wonderful fiction books available that are not on these lists. I gave preference to authors of series books or to authors who have written many similar books, so if your child likes my suggestions, you can find other similar books. The title for each author that I list is a favorite of my students, but usually if kids like one book by an author, they'll like others as well.

Note that when I indicate a series, your child can probably read the books in that series in any order. They are usually formula-written and very easy to read. When I list a title and add "plus sequels," you should start with the title I list, as the subsequent ones are dependent on the first one. These books are usually not formula-written and are often harder and more complex to read.

Books or series that are especially easy, or especially interesting to kids who dislike reading, I've starred (*). My division of some sections into younger and older readers should be taken only as an approximation, since I find interest matters much more than reading level. Generally, however, I think of younger readers as being between seven or eight and twelve, and older readers as teenagers. But there's always much overlap.

More information on most of these authors, as well as student comments evaluating their books, are included in my first book, *Parents Who Love Reading, Kids Who Don't.*

FAMILY AND FRIEND BOOKS THAT ARE OPTIMISTIC, IMAGINATIVE, AND USUALLY END HAPPILY

Younger Readers

1 **American Girls series**. Various authors. These are novels that describe the adventures of young girls during different historical periods. The Pleasant Company also sells a line of dolls modeled after these main characters.

*2 **Berenstain, Stan and Jan**. Berenstain Bear series. There are both picture books and chapter books in this incredibly popular series. Kids like the gently humorous picture of family life.

3 **Burnett, Frances Hodgson**. *The Secret Garden*. Poignant story set in Victorian England that is still loved by my high school seniors.

4

Cleary, Beverly. *Ramona* plus sequels, as well as many other similar books. Gently comic tales of children who *try* to be good.

5

Lovelace, Maud Hart. *Betsy-Tacy* plus sequels. A series set in turn-of-the-century Minnesota, much loved by girls, first published in the 1940s. All are in paperback now.

*6

Martin, Ann M. The Babysitters Club series. Many, many titles about how friends help each other. There is also a Babysitters Little Sister series for very young readers.

7

Montgomery, L. M. *Anne of Green Gables* plus sequels. The books are even better than the excellent PBS series.

*8

Pascal, Francine. Sweet Valley series, which describe the happy lives of twins from early childhood (Sweet Valley Kids) to college (Sweet Valley University). Hundreds of titles.

9 Taylor, Sydney: All-of-a-Kind Family series. Five little girls living with their parents at the turn of the century in New York.

Older Readers

10 Binchy, Maeve. *Circle of Friends,* which is only one of a number of her books about life in small Irish villages.

11 Pilcher, Rosamunde. *Coming Home,* and many more warm, nonformula romances set in England.

*12 Steel, Danielle. *The Promise,* plus many, many novels about glamorous, strong heroines who overcome troubles and find love.

MORE REALISTIC, PROBLEM-CENTERED FAMILY AND FRIEND BOOKS

Younger Readers

13 Paterson, Katherine. *Bridge to Terabithia,* plus similar books that deal sympathetically with serious problems in the lives of young girls.

14 Taylor, Mildred. *Roll of Thunder, Hear My Cry,* plus sequel. Classic stories of African American children coming of age in the South during the first part of this century.

Older Readers

***15** Blume, Judy. *Forever.* This is the one book I've never had a teenage girl not finish.

16 Campbell, Bebe Moore. *Brothers and Sisters,* plus other novels of African Americans dealing with contemporary problems.

17 Conroy, Pat. *The Prince of Tides,* and other beautifully written, bitterly funny stories of family dysfunction.

18 Cormier, Robert. *The Chocolate War* is one of a number of short novels about teenagers involved in life-and-death situations.

*19 Hinton, S. E. *The Outsiders,* plus four more very, very popular, easy-to-read stories of teenagers on their own. Almost infallible books for the nonreading teen.

*20 McMillan, Terry. *Disappearing Acts,* plus more novels about how strong, funny African American women deal with the men in their lives. Almost infallible books for the black teenage girl.

21 Salinger, J. D. *Catcher in the Rye* is the all-time-classic tragicomic coming-of-age story of Holden Caulfield wandering through New York. Salinger has a few other books that are almost as popular.

22 Tan, Amy. *The Joy Luck Club* is one of her novels about the lives of Chinese American immigrants.

23 Voight, Cynthia. *Dicey's Song* and other teenage novels about neglected children coping on their own.

24 Walker, Alice. *The Color Purple* is by far her most popular story of African American women becoming strong, but she does have some other titles.

MYSTERIES THAT ARE COMIC OR INTRIGUING RATHER THAN SCARY

Younger Readers

*25 Choose Your Own Adventure books by various authors. Easy reading. A good way to move kids into chapter books.

26 Dadey, Debbie et al. Adventures of the Bailey School Kids series. Comic and easy to read.

27 Dixon, Franklin W. The Hardy Boys series. Scores of titles and still very popular.

28 Keene, Caroline. Nancy Drew series. Mysteries with a strong heroine and scores of titles.

29 Warner, Gertrude Chandler. The Boxcar Children series. More than fifty titles and very popular.

Older Readers

30 **Grafton, Sue.** *"A" Is for Alibi,* plus many more titles in this series about a tough, smart woman detective.

31 **Grisham, John.** *The Firm* started the craze for lawyer mysteries. Kids like his other books too.

32 **Hillerman, Tony.** *The Dark Wind,* plus more mysteries that feature a Navajo detective.

33 **Cussler, Clive.** *Pacific Vortex* is one of many of Cussler's action books set in wild nature settings. Kids tell me his early novels are the best. He's especially popular with boys who also like survival and hunting stories.

*34 **Parker, Robert B.** Spenser series. Funny, fast-moving, easy-reading detective stories set in Boston.

THRILLERS AND HORROR BOOKS THAT ARE VERY SUSPENSEFUL AND SOMETIMES SCARY

Younger Readers

35 Bellairs, John. *The Chessmen of Doom* is just one of his suspenseful and fast-moving tales.

36 Pike, Christopher. Last Vampire series in addition to many more books. Pike is second only to Stine in kids' horror.

*37 Stine, R. L. Goosebumps series. The current best-selling children's author by far. Kids love his books. The covers are lurid, but the stories deliver a safe scare. His Fear Street series is for older readers.

Older Readers

*38   **Andrews, V. C.** *Flowers in the Attic,* plus sequels, as well as several other series. Andrews is the best bet for that teenage girl who can't get through books.

39   **Clark, Mary Higgins.** *Remember Me* is one of her many books, all equally popular, that show women in perilous situations.

40   **Crichton, Michael.** *Congo* is a favorite, but boys, especially, like all his high-tech suspense thrillers.

41   **King, Stephen.** *The Shining,* I'm told by kids, is the best, but my students like all his books.

42   **Koontz, Dean R.** *Icebound* is one of a number of his books that are like Stephen King's, but often contain a psychic element.

*43 Patterson, James. *Along Came a Spider,* plus sequels. This series, which features a tough, engaging African American detective, is a must try for black teenage boys.

44 Rice, Anne. *The Witching Hour,* plus sequels, as well as another series featuring vampires. Rice is the queen of horror, and writes rich, complex, image-filled novels.

SCIENCE FICTION AND FANTASY BOOKS

Younger Readers

45 Coville, Bruce. *Aliens Ate My Homework,* plus other funny books about aliens. Comic and easy to read.

46 L'Engle, Madeleine. *A Wrinkle in Time,* and sequels. Rich, imaginative fantasy.

47 Lewis, C. S. *The Lion, the Witch and the Wardrobe,* plus sequels, which make up the Narnia series. Girls who love magic and pretending also love this series.

48 Yolen, Jane. *Dragon's Blood,* plus sequels, for middle grade children, and Commander Toad books for very young readers.

Older Readers

49 Adams, Douglas. *The Hitchiker's Guide to the Galaxy,* plus sequels. Absurd, sophomoric humor kids love.

*50 Anthony, Piers. *A Spell for Chameleon,* plus sequels. Anthony also wrote many other complex, much-loved fantasy series.

*51 Asprin, Robert. The Myth series. Short, funny fantasy books that are a good entry into fantasy for older readers.

52 Brooks, Terry. Shannara series. Lengthy dragon and sword books. Very popular with junior-high boys.

53 Card, Orson Scott. *Ender's Game,* plus sequels. The absolute favorite science fiction series of many readers.

54 Eddings, David. The Belgariad series is the most popular of his fantasies, and are a good entry into fantasy reading for teens.

*55 Forgotten Realms series. Various authors, many titles, often trilogies. Easy to read and very popular.

56 Jordan, Robert. His Wheel of Time series is very sophisticated fantasy, much loved by top readers. His Conan books are a little easier.

57 Tolkien, J.R.R. *Lord of the Rings.* Tolkien set the standard for modern fantasy, and his books are still incredibly popular.

58 Weis, Margaret, and Tracy Hickman. The Dragonlance Chronicles. Other writers have taken over the series, but the early ones by Weis and Hickman are the best.

MAGIC BOOKS (LIGHTER IN TONE AND DEALING MORE WITH INTERPERSONAL RELATIONSHIPS THAN TRADITIONAL FANTASY DOES)

Younger Readers

59 Banks, Lynne Reid. *The Indian in the Cupboard,* plus sequels. An Indian figure comes alive. Girls who like dolls like these.

60 Cole, Joanna. Magic School Bus series. Kids travel and learn science in these stories.

*61   **Dahl, Roald.** *Charlie and the Chocolate Factory* is just one of his dazzling adventures that kids love. Dahl is perhaps the most-loved children's author.

62   **Eager, Edward.** *Half Magic* and several sequels. Magical adventures of four British children.

63   **Jacques, Brian.** *Redwall,* plus sequels. About abbey mice battling evil through the generations. Rich, complex fantasy that is read by kids up through high school.

64   Magic Attic Club series by various authors. Beautifully illustrated books about little girls who dress up in an attic and pretend to be all kinds of different characters. Easy reading.

65   **Nesbit, E.** *The Railway Children,* plus many more novels by this much-loved British author.

MILITARY/WAR/PILOT BOOKS

Older Readers

66 Berent, Mark. *Rolling Thunder* plus sequels are stories of Air Force pilots during the Vietnam War.

67 Clancy, Tom. *The Hunt for Red October* is the first of his many long novels that are famous for their realistic military details.

68 Coonts, Stephen. *Flight of the Intruder* plus more novels that follow the adventures of navy pilots during and after Vietnam.

69 Cornwell, Bernard. The Richard Sharp books take place during the Napoleonic wars, and the Starbuck Chronicles take place during the U.S. Civil War.

70 DeMille, Nelson. *Cathedral* is one of his thrillers, whose varied subject matter ranges from the Irish Republican Army to Vietnam to Russia to organized crime.

71 Griffin, W.E.B. Brotherhood of War series, which portrays army and marine officers from pre–WWII through Vietnam.

BALLET

72 Costello, Emily, and Marcy Ramsey. Ballet School series written for middle grade readers.

HORSEBACK RIDING

73 Betancourt, Jeanne. Pony Pals. New series for very young readers.

*74 Bryant, Bonnie. The Saddle Club series has more than fifty titles so far and is very popular.

75 Campbell, Joanna. The Thoroughbred series is her most popular, but she has written many other books as well.

76 Farley, Walter. *The Black Stallion* and sequels. Classic horse stories.

77 Francis, Dick. *Bonecrack,* plus many more suspense stories set in the world of horse racing. Try these with teenagers.

HUNTING, CAMPING, SURVIVAL

78 Eckert, Allan W. *Incidents of Hawk's Hill* is about a boy, in 1870, who gets lost in the wild and forms an alliance with a badger. Eckert has written other nature titles as well.

79 George, Jean Craighead. *Julie of the Wolves,* plus sequel. These are only two of her beautifully written survival stories.

80 Kjelgaard, Jim. *Big Red* plus sequels and other books about hunting.

81 Mowat, Farley. *Never Cry Wolf* is only one of his many true stories about wild animals.

82 O'Dell, Scott. *Island of the Blue Dolphins*. A classic tale about using nature to survive.

*83 Paulsen, Gary. *Hatchet* and many other books about hunting and survival. His books are a must try for boys who like the outdoors.

84 Rawls, Wilson. *Where the Red Fern Grows,* a story of a boy and his hunting dogs, is one of the best-loved books of all time.

85 Speare, Elizabeth George. *The Sign of the Beaver* is just one of her wonderful nature books. It's about a boy who has to survive a winter in the Maine woods in the 1700s and makes friends with an Indian tribe.

SPORTS

*86   **Christopher, Matt.** *Face-Off* plus many books about baseball, hockey, basketball, and soccer. The ball on each book's spine shows what sport the book is about.

87   **Dygard, Thomas J.** *Quarterback Walk-On* as well as books on soccer, basketball, baseball, and camping.

88   **Edwards, T. J.** Sports Mystery series. A new series of books on basketball, baseball, football, and soccer.

89   **Hughes, Dean.** Various Angel Park series. Hughes has different series for different sports—so far a baseball, football, and soccer series.

BASEBALL

90 Freeman, Mark. Rookies series. A new series about the Rosemont High School team.

BASKETBALL

91 Herman, Hank. Super Hoops series. A brand-new series about the Branford Bulls.

92 Marshall, Kirk. Hoops series. Brian moves and has to compete with inner-city basketball players.

*93 Meyers, Walter Dean. *Hoops,* plus sequel, as well as other stories about black inner-city players.

GYMNASTICS

94 **Charbonnet, Gabrielle.** American Gold Gymnasts series. A new series inspired by the 1996 Olympics, about rivalries and friendships among some top young gymnasts.

95 **Slater, Teddy, and Wayne Alfano.** Junior Gymnasts series, a new series about friendship problems among a group of young gymnasts. Good for young readers.

HOCKEY

96 **Brouwer, Sigmund.** Lightning on Ice, a new series for middle grade readers.

97 **O'Connor, Jim** et al. The No Stars. A new series about young hockey players who have to learn to deal with a girl on their team.

ICE SKATING

98 Lowell, Melissa. The Silver Blades series is a long series with about eighteen titles so far. The stories are mostly about friendship and competition on the ice.

99 Older, Effin. Silver Blades Figure Eights is a new series for very young readers.

SWIMMING

100 Wyeth, Sharon Dennis. American Gold Swimmers is a new series featuring the friendships and first loves of girls on a swimming team.

ABOUT THE AUTHOR

Mary Leonhardt, the author of *Parents Who Love Reading, Kids Who Don't* and *Keeping Kids Reading,* has taught English in public, private, and parochial schools for twenty-five years. She is currently at Concord-Carlisle High School in Massachusetts.